HOW
TO BUY
A HOUSE
IN AUSTIN

Kristina Modares

This book was part of the inspiration for the creation of Open House Austin, a real estate educational hub and community event center in East Austin. Open House Austin was created to build an inclusive community around local business, finances, real estate, and activism. We support others with their pursuits, while building connections and community around first time home buyers.

3307 Oak Spring Dr. Austin, TX 78721

OpenHouseAustin.co

@OpenHouse_Austin

Introduction

I vividly remember the day I first searched for my own home. A recent graduate, I had just moved to Austin, Texas, after deciding that I needed a change. I left the city I grew up in, thinking it would help me develop into the person I knew I wanted to be, but I still didn't know what direction I wanted to take in life. Was I in the right career? Did I surround myself with good company? Was I living a fulfilling life? A classic case of yet another confused 20-something year old. Then, I began to read business, management, and self-help books. I realized I could fulfill my big-picture dreams through real estate, and I wanted others to know they may benefit from it as well. This informational guide is intended to shed some light on a process that most of us don't learn in school. Some of you reading this may know more now than I did at 23 years old. However, it never hurts to educate yourself further before you make one of the most significant financial and personal decisions of your life: buying a home. Here you will be provided with a basic outline to walk you through the process. It will give you a better understanding of what to look for when purchasing your first home in Austin.

--Kristina Modares

Bottom Line: Don't overcomplicate this. If you are ready, willing, and able to buy a home, waiting will only hurt you in the long run. We all fear the unknown, and no matter how much information you collect, you'll never really know everything until you go out and experience it for yourself.

Disclaimer: A lot of the information provided is based on my personal experience as an Austin resident and real estate agent.

Table of Contents

Why Should I Buy A House?............................5
Why Work With Open House Austin?...............12
Okay! You've Convinced Me. 16
Step #1. Assemble a Kick-Ass Real Estate Team........17
Step #2. Identify and Fulfill Wants & Needs.................26
Step #3. BINGO! Found The One...............................28
Step #4. Submit an Offer...31
Step #5. Yay! Offer Accepted.....................................42
Step #6. Pre-closure: I See the Light!..........................46
Step #7. Final Walk Through: The Home Stretch!........48
Step #8. Closing Time...49
Step #9. Celebrate!...50
Common Questions and Concerns..............................51
Austin Activity Starter Kit...64

Why Should I Buy a House?

Are you paying a ton on rent? Do you plan on sticking around Austin for a while? Do you have a stable job? Then the answer is easy. You probably can and should buy. I'll tell you why. You should be putting your money into your own home, not into something you rent temporarily! If you live in Austin, you're paying too much in rent each month and throwing away hard earned cash. Odds are, your monthly mortgage payment will be less or about the same as what you pay in rent. With a stable job, loan approval will be easier to obtain, and that's half the battle.

Before you start looking at houses, evaluate your personal and financial situation. Not everyone reading this needs to buy a property. Depending on your financial and personal circumstances and how you intend to create a better lifestyle for yourself and your loved ones. Everyone wants homeownership for different reasons. I noticed that the people I considered successful owned at least one property, and I wanted to find out the reasons why.

Reason Number One: Rent is the worst. Yes, shelter is one of your basic needs, but does that basic need have to eat away at 15-30% of your yearly earnings? You are throwing away money each month while leasing. Many people in Austin are paying $1,800 or more in rent every

5

month. That is $21,600 a year that you will never see again. Instead of throwing away $1,800 or more each month on rent, you could own a property with a $1,800 fixed monthly payment AND gain equity on your property. Equity is the amount of money you have put into your property and what you get back when you sell it. Remember, rent increases with inflation, but your mortgage payment is fixed! Some may argue that your taxes could go up each year, changing your monthly payment a bit. There are ways to challenge these increases and keep your taxes from increasing too much each year.

Reason Number Two: Control. When you own the property that you live in, you call the shots. Owning a house guarantees the absence of property managers and landlords; thus, no more people telling you what you can and can't do. I like the fact that I can utilize Airbnb during events like SXSW to get extra cash. Want to paint your walls? Do it. Want to plant a garden in the yard? Go for it! Want a trampoline in your backyard? Why the hell not?! I don't know about you, but I want the freedom to do projects in my house without somebody breathing down my neck.

To some people, the control is the scariest part about owning a home. Many first time buyers tell me they want to buy a condo instead of a single-family home because they are afraid of the maintenance that they assume comes with a single-family home. I compare buying property to enrolling in an educational program or grad school. How many hours of education do you want to tack on in this chapter of your life? When you buy a home or a condo, you not only get shelter, but you also get an excellent education. New experiences can be intimidating, but I can't explain to you the amount of confidence you receive after dealing with a few home repairs on your own. Even the act of hiring and dealing with contractors is a fantastic learning experience. If you're still a little uneasy about home repairs, a condo or townhouse may be the right path for you. That path may fit better into the lifestyle that you're trying to sustain. Self-awareness is key in not only deciding what kind of property to buy but in determining if buying is even right for you!

Reason Number Three: Passive Income through rental properties. Passive income is income received regularly, with little effort required to maintain it. Passive income is a great retirement plan, especially when you don't have a pension. Start saving now! When I started looking into real estate investing, I discovered that the common denominator of successful people is making their money work for them. Many of them did this through real estate. Want to have a career and family with time left for friends, traveling, and community involvement? Yeah, me too! Work less, make more money, and have more time. Whether that be spending time with your family, getting involved in your community, or drinking a margarita at the beach on a Monday afternoon. Although your first home may not be an investment property, it will get you more familiar with the real estate world, and possibly one step closer in that direction.

Why Austin?

Safe Bet

Austin has exhibited exemplary growth in the past couple of decades. Homes have appreciated an average of ten percent per year in the past ten years, which is five percent greater than the national average. If you study a chart of growth, it looks more like a stair step than lateral ups and downs, which is usually shown with market crashes.

Austin's economy is highly resilient, even during national economic crises. For example, in the 2008 Great Recession, Austin's home prices stayed flat, while most other cities experienced massive crashes and home price drops. A few theories arose as to why the Texas economy fared better in the 2008 recession:

One: Texas got a late start in the recession. 2008 was a period of high energy prices, and Texas saw a pretty significant energy boom as well.

Two: The high-tech industry provided a bit of a buffer. When energy prices finally did fall as the recession picked up steam, Texas' economy declined slower than the national average, and then bounced back faster.

Three: Some people theorize it was because many banks and lenders held steady onto their conservative and un-exotic lending practices.

Four: People also attribute it to a lowered cost of land and utilities throughout Texas, thus holding down the cost of living. Regardless, Austin and the rest of Texas fared well.

Austin attracts startup and tech companies, driving the local economy. It remains more affordable than the tech-driven markets on the coasts. For many businesses, the Texas Capital has just what they need: a skilled technology workforce and a comparatively lower cost of living. Also, Austin has one of the lowest unemployment rates nationwide

Progressive City Vibe Without The Cost Nor The Attitude
Those who have lived in Austin for many years will comment about the increase in costs. However, if you compare it to other progressive cities from where people may move—like San Francisco, New York City, Boston—Austin is much more affordable. Millennials are finally more prominently participating in the home buyers market, which highlights the affordable housing issue. Recently, Austin is addressing this more seriously. That doesn't mean there isn't affordable housing available; it may just be harder to find. That's where a proactive real estate agent comes in handy!

If you look at other progressive cities, Austin is definitely on the cheaper side of the spectrum. The average home cost in Austin (2016) is in the mid $300's, whereas in the similar cities mentioned above, the average costs can be in the $700s.

Also, Austin has a more laid back environment. Most people don't drive flashy cars or wear expensive suits and stilettos. People are active socially and physically, and there is a very comfortable and low-key vibe. In Austin, there is relief for those escaping the flashy lifestyle of say, Silicon Valley. Some Austinites rip on people moving from California because of that stigma. I'm hopeful that the new surge in West Coasters won't change Austin for the worst. It probably means more people want to adapt to this lifestyle. Fingers crossed.

Why Work With Open House Austin?

Open House Austin was founded by my business partner Steph Douglass and me in December 2018. We are a female-owned real estate team at Realty Austin, the largest independent Brokerage in Austin, and we are working on expanding the possibilities of home ownership in Austin, TX. I wanted to share the following resources that we provide all of our clients because I know it can be hard to pick a realtor in town. There are so many of us, and this is a huge milestone and a big deal! I want to show you how much we care about our clients and how we set them up to succeed. If our message is speaking to you, hopefully, we will have the opportunity to work together in the future. Steph and I would love to be your realtors!

Open House Austin Resources:

1. How To Buy a House in Austin:
This book...you're reading it! Before I was a real estate agent, I was shopping for homes and was not getting the guidance and knowledge I needed to make me feel secure with such a huge purchase. I realized there was not enough transparency around buying a house. My agent showed me homes but did not guide me on anything else. When I did find a house I loved, I couldn't even purchase it because I didn't have a preapproval

letter, and I lost out on the house. After that horrible experience, I realized that no one was catering to first-time buyers. That's when I decided to get my license and write this book. This book goes through the entire process of buying a house and helps our clients get a head start on their home search. As your realtors, we will be walking you through each step along the way,---our book is just a tool to make you feel a bit more prepared. It will be much less overwhelming if you have a general idea of what you're walking into before you go under contract on a house.

2. Monthly Workshops For First Time Home Buyers

Ninety-five percent of our clients are first time buyers who are worried about their lack of knowledge and what that means about their ability to make a smart purchase. When you hear conflicting information from all angles, it's hard to feel confident in yourself as a buyer! Our monthly buyer workshops are held at our space in East Austin at 3307 Oak Springs Dr. We purposely create an intimate setting so you will feel comfortable to ask questions, state your hesitations, and address misconceptions. We walk buyers through the many steps of buying a house and simplify the process so that it doesn't feel as daunting. You'll leave with confidence in your ability to buy a home, a badass real estate team, and your next steps to homeownership.

3. Homeowner Support Group

Maybe the thought of buying your first home seems scary because you no longer have a landlord to call to fix things. And how will you know what to do if things go awry? Steph and I don't go away after you officially become a homeowner. You will have us to help answer questions throughout the year. We also created a homeowner Facebook group for our clients. It's a great resource and a place to share questions, concerns, and homeowner wins! Clients will share their renovation stories, who their favorite contractors are, and also tips on how they saved money on their property taxes. Steph and I often post valuable articles and events. We founded Open House Austin to create a supportive community for our clients and neighbors. We realize that it can be scary to be a homeowner, and we want our clients to feel confident and secure.

4. Investment & Renovation Consultation:

We also offer investment and renovation consultation. We are experienced real estate investors and have overseen multiple renovations. We know how houses are built, we have a good idea of what things cost, and we have an eye for potential. We love helping clients see the vision of a space, but at the same time, we have experience with big-ticket home fixes and can help you assess how much of a project you'd like to take on. A lot of our clients don't want a project at all! Which makes it even more important to know the warning signs of imminent homeowner threats. We calm the nerves of future homeowners by being well-informed and experienced. We know working with contractors feels scary, which is why we have an ever-growing list of reputable contractors who we've worked with and can recommend. This will prevent you from having to turn to the vast darkness of the internet for home help.

Okay! You've Convinced Me. How Do I Buy a House?

Below are the basic steps you need to consider when buying a home in Austin.

1. Assemble a Kick-Ass Real Estate Team.

2. Identify and Fulfill Wants and Needs.

3. BINGO. Found The One!

4. Submit an Offer.

5. Yay! Offer Accepted.
       (Or)
    Dang. Back To The Drawing Board.

6. Pre-closure: I See The Light.

7. Final Walk Through: The Home Stretch!

8. Closing Time.

9. Celebrate!

Step #1. Assemble a Kick-Ass Real Estate Team.

I want to emphasize the importance of this step. If you do this correctly, buying a house will be so much easier. Your "Real Estate Team" is made up of your real estate agent, lender, and title company. Agents should be willing to go the distance for their clients to help them buy their dream home. You need to find someone you're compatible with and somebody easy to get ahold of even after you go under contract. I can't stress enough how important it is for all parties to be in sync. Excellent communication and responsiveness from everyone, including you, the buyer, will ensure the process runs as smoothly as possible. This is a machine that won't function properly if one gear isn't greased.

Start with a Real Estate Agent

You should ALWAYS have a real estate agent by your side, especially as a buyer. Why? To protect yourself! Find a real estate agent who will represent your best interests. You need someone that can speak eloquently on your behalf when you are not present. You want someone who will stand up for you and further negotiate if the seller pushes back about repairs you've requested. You need someone who will consistently look out for your financial interests and keep you up to date on the success of the transaction. This is the BIGGEST and MOST IMPORTANT reason everyone should get a real estate agent. The reality is some buyers' agents will do a lot, and some won't do much at all. There are so many real estate agents in Austin. You need to make sure that you're working with somebody you feel comfortable with.

What Your Real Estate Agent Should Do For You:
- Be your free guide and counselor through the whole process.
- Communicate with the lender, title company, and seller so that you're able to close on time.
- Clearly communicate with you throughout the transaction and answer all questions or, if they can't, find somebody who can.
- Help you analyze price and value, and help you come up with a negotiating strategy.
- Accompany you during inspections. Assist in interpreting inspection results and negotiating inspection issues.
- Someone to buffer you from pushy sellers, the sellers real estate agent, and anyone else who is not looking out for your best interests.
- Build your ideal Real Estate Team.
- Connect you with service providers—inspectors, lenders, home warranty companies.
- Educate and update you on the purchase process.
- Provide listings for homes meeting your criteria.

- Organize showing appointments. Schedule and show you homes.

Remember, a buyer's agent's services are **FREE TO BUYERS.** This should be the first step in your home buying process because you should start using this free resource as soon as possible. It is the real estate agent's responsibility to guide you in the right direction. So, find somebody that you work well with and trust to get the answers you need!

The seller's agent works for the seller and represents them in the transaction. A seller pays both the buyer's agent and seller's agent's commission. I've provided an example below.

Example of How a Real Estate Agent Gets Paid:
Sales Price: **$235,000**. In this example, the seller has agreed to pay their real estate agent a commission of 6 percent of the sales price. The sellers agent agrees that 3 percent of this will go to the buyer's agent.

Total Commission Paid by Seller:
$235,000 * 6%= **$14,100**.

Seller's Agent: $14,100/2= **$7,050**.

Buyer's Agent: $14,100/2= **$7,050**.

The buyer's agent and seller's agent usually have to give a cut of their commission to their broker. The percentage of the cut differs between each brokerage. The agent also pays for their own business expenses and taxes.

Next Find a Lender

The second member of your team! You should contact a lender before searching for an Austin home. This is because you'll need to know what your budget is before making specific decisions such as where to buy, how many bedrooms, features, etc. Let's say you have your heart set on living in the hot, South Austin zip code, 78704. You start looking online at three bedroom homes and notice that the average list price is $600,000. After months of searching, you finally speak to a lender and realize that your actual budget is $400,000 max. At this point, you need to reevaluate your whole plan. Maybe you start searching further south? Maybe you start looking at condos? Bottom line: **know your budget before you go shopping**. Trust me. Nothing hurts like finding your dream home and realizing it cannot be yours.

How Do I Find a Good Lender?

The best way to find a reputable lender is to ask around. Start with your realtor; they work with many different lenders and can help you find someone right for you. Another useful resource would be to ask your network and talk to people you like and trust who have recently bought a house. What was their experience?

I think working with a local lender or credit union is a much better experience than a big bank, and they will take the time to explain your options and go over the lending process. I do not recommend big banks as they tend to over promise and under deliver. I often give my buyers a few contacts to reach out to and tell them to shop rates. If you have a great experience with the first lender but received a better rate from the second person you talked to, don't shy away from asking the first lender to match the other lender's rate! They will often do it, and then you get a great rate and work with someone you enjoy communicating with.

Questions You May Want to Ask Your Lender:
- What will my mortgage payments look like if I put 5 or 10 percent down vs a 20 percent down payment?
- How much money will I need to come up with to buy a home?
- How long will my pre-approval letter last?
- What kinds of mortgages should I consider?
- What will my mortgage cover?
- How can I quickly raise my credit score?

Why Should I Talk To a Lender Before Shopping?
Working with a lender shows that you are a serious buyer. We often put off this step because it's not nearly as exciting as browsing pictures of homes and envisioning a future there. The truth is, you can look online all day, but

put it on the list of other ways we waste time, next to Instagram scrolling, Pinterest browsing, and Netflix binging. Don't mistake looking online for productive house searching.

You need to talk to a lender before shopping because:
- You need realistic expectations. For example, if you make $40,000 a year, you may not be able to afford a $300,000 home by yourself. Your lender will tell you what your budget is and what you need to do to get into something within your budget.
- You need a pre-approval letter to show sellers that you're a serious buyer when making offers.
- You should start learning about loan approval ASAP and begin to form a relationship with your lender. This way, you won't feel lost when it comes to making an offer.
- The sooner you start the paperwork, the sooner it will be over. You need to start collecting documents for your lender to review so that you can get pre-approved.

A lender will also let you know what you need to do to get approved. It may be as simple as fixing a minor credit issue that you thought was a huge deal. I've worked with clients who were very hesitant about contacting a lender because they were scared of what they might hear. After I had put them in touch with a great lender, they realized what they needed to do to fix their financial situation and were approved quickly.

What is This Lender Person Going to Need From Me?
*The lender may ask for additional information
- Copies of your checking and savings account statements for the past six months
  - Lenders look through hundreds of statements; don't think they will sit there and analyze everything on which you spend your money. It's like going to the doctor—they've seen it all
- Credit score and history
  - You don't have to have a perfect credit score. Many lenders can even work with people with a score around 580. Even if your score is too low, they will give you tips on how to improve your number.
- Recent paycheck stub, detailing your earnings
  - A lender decides how much you can afford by reviewing your income stability and monthly income.
- Social security number
- All credit card accounts and the approximate monthly amounts owed on each
- Account numbers and balances due on outstanding loans, i.e. your student loans
- Income tax statements from the last two years

- Someone who can verify your employment—most likely your supervisor/boss

A Pre-approval Letter is a document you must have when ready to submit offers if you want to be taken seriously as a buyer. They usually last anywhere between 60-120 days. To get a pre-approval letter, you'll complete a mortgage application and provide your lender with all the necessary documentation. This is very important. Remember, they are about to lend you a lot of money and need to make sure you are capable of paying it back! With less information, you can get "pre-qualified" instead of "pre-approved," but sellers would rather work with a "pre-approved buyer" over a "pre-qualified buyer." This is because there is less risk that the deal will fall through. If your lender gathers all this information from you once you go under contract, instead of before, they may find you actually cannot afford the home you put an offer on. STRONG BUYERS ARE PRE-APPROVED.

Down Payments Today, 40 percent of buyers put down less than 10 percent, and many put down as little as 3 percent. Your lender can show you what your payments will look like monthly and long-term if you put down 5 vs. 10 vs. 20 percent. Even if you end up paying PMI now, you can usually cancel it when you have paid the mortgage balance to 80 percent of the home's appraised value. Your lender can better explain how you can cancel PMI, based on your situation.

When it comes to down payments, I've found that many people are misinformed. They think that it's required to put down 20 percent of the sales price; this is FALSE. While it is true that if you don't put down 20 percent, you will have to pay Private Mortgage Insurance, it still may make sense financially to buy now, rather than wait until you have the 20 percent. After all, you still give money to a landlord every month. Interest rates are historically very low, and now more than ever, it makes sense to many buyers to put little money down.

Private Mortgage Insurance, or PMI, is a monthly fee anywhere between .05 percent to 5 percent of the principal amount of the loan. This fee protects the lender in case you default on your monthly mortgage payment. This amount is also included in your monthly mortgage payment, so you are not required to make multiple payments a month.

Step #2. Identify and Fulfill Wants & Needs.

After you know what you can afford, you can begin to think about your deal breakers.

Typical "deal breakers" I commonly see with clients include:

- Distance from downtown
- School districts (GreatSchools.org is a good resource)
- Move-in ready
- "I want chickens in my yard and will the Homeowners Association allow my micro pig?"

Okay, the last one isn't common, but it's definitely been asked!

I provide clients with more in-depth stats on schooling and neighborhoods when I get to know them as individuals. As soon as I know their character, combined with their deal breakers, I can help them narrow down an area.

Consider your needs as well:

- Do you work from home and need an office?
- Do you want roommates to help cover your mortgage payment?
- Do you need to live close to work?

Physically writing out a list of your wants and needs will not only help you to better understand what you're looking for but also help your real estate agent find the best matches for you, saving you both time and energy.

Those who don't know much about the Austin market think that to buy a single family home, they need to be willing to spend $500,000. Not the case! You can still find reasonably priced homes in the Austin area; you just won't be 5 minutes from downtown.

Step #3. BINGO! Found The One.

In Austin, looking at homes in person too early will be, quite frankly, pointless. I suggest looking online first to get a feel for what's on the market and what's selling quickly or sitting longer. Set up a home search to do this and monitor it daily or even weekly. Be careful which online service you use; Zillow and Trulia don't always have updated information, and hundreds of real estate agents use it as a lead generation source. Meaning, if you inquire about a home, your phone may start buzzing for a few days.

If you enjoy looking at homes in person, check out open houses. Ask your real estate agent for a list of upcoming open houses in your area of interest and hop around one weekend. You can also use our website (OpenHouseAustin.co), to find them yourself and set up a home search. Make sure you let the agent hosting the open house know that you already have a real estate agent. Many real estate agents hold open houses for lead generation, and they may try to win you over as a client. If you let them know ahead of time, it will save you both time and energy.

About three to five months from when you need to move into your new home, start getting more serious in your search. Remember to keep in mind; you may need a longer or shorter search period, depending on your situation. You'll now visit the homes you're interested in with your agent. They will also send you information on homes that have recently sold in the neighborhood. This way, you'll have a clear idea of how quickly homes are appreciating in that particular area, and see if the home for sale is overpriced by comparison. Your agent should also contact the listing agent and get more information, possibly not shared online. Your agent will come in handy and provide inaccessible market information. They can even pull the history of the home, including the last time it was sold, and also explain questions you may have. For example, "Hmm, why was this property listed on the market last month, and then it went pending, and then it came back on the market multiple times. Is this a red flag?"

For quite some time now, Austin has had low inventory. One reason is because of the low level of new housing builds. While recovering from the 2008 recession, most builders were unable to start new developments. Another issue in Austin is getting past the city and its permit hurdles, including restrictions, labor, administration, and costs. Often, this has resulted in a much slower start-to-finish build cycle. Although this may seem like bad news for a buyer, real estate is continually changing, and

Austin is seeing more and more new construction popping up everywhere, despite past permit and builder issues.

How many homes should you view before finding "The One"? Consider this: how many dates should you go on before the first kiss? There is no right answer; you will just know. I once showed a couple ONE home, they fell in love, and put an offer on it the next day. Finding what you're looking for may take less time than you'd think.

Because of technology and being able to look online, you may find you only look at a few homes before deciding to make an offer. Or, you do the opposite and spend a month looking. Whatever your method, don't let your emotions get in the way of seeing great potential in a home or get too attached when you put in an offer. Looking at houses can be fun, but this isn't HGTV. Reality will hit hard if you over-complicate your search, let your emotions take control, or shop before knowing what you can afford. A little education goes a long way!

Step #4. Submit an Offer.

Filling out the necessary paperwork and waiting for it to be reviewed can cause a little anxiety. Yet, when you're going through the motions with a real estate agent by your side, the task will not seem so daunting. Your agent will prep you as best as they can. Don't fret! An excellent agent walks clients step by step through this process and makes sure everything is done correctly.

When you submit an offer there are a few documents that you will need besides the sales contract:

- **Contract.** I will go over this in the next section
- **Third party financing addendum.** If you use a lender/bank, this document is required. This document states what type of financing you have (Conventional, FHA, or VA loan). It also says how many days you, as a buyer, have to get financing. If you don't get financing within those days, you can back out of the contract and get your earnest money back. We go over earnest money in the next section.
- **Pre-approval letter.** This is a letter that you get from your lender or bank. You may be thinking, "Doesn't that mean I already have financing? Why do I need a third party financing addendum?" A pre-approval is NOT final approval. It just means your lender has enough information and you should qualify for a particular loan

amount based upon what you have provided. The determination and loan amount is based on income and credit information that you have given them. So, if you are leaving out information or if you buy a car when you go under contract, you may be denied financing.

- **Sellers Disclosure.** This is a document completed by the seller of a home. It lists any known issues with the property, as well as any remodeling projects done during the time they owned the home. The seller doesn't have to report any problem that they are unaware of. If you buy the house and discover a problem, how can you tell whether the owner knew about it? That's why you hire a home inspector. We will go over that next.

Breaking Down a Standard Real Estate Contract

Let's now discuss the contract for submitting an offer. Keep in mind; Texas State attorneys created the contract, not a real estate agent or broker. Most residential real estate contracts in Texas use the standard Texas Real Estate Commission contract. I would suggest going to their website and talking to a lawyer if you have any specific legal questions. A contract to buy a property is pretty standard, but there are a few versions, depending on if you purchase a new home, condo, farm/ranch, etc. Each of these contracts is different.

The following section will show different parts of a standard contract and go over them, briefly. You can go to https://www.trec.state.tx.us to read through a complete copy.

■ Sales price

3. **SALES PRICE:**
   A. Cash portion of Sales Price payable by Buyer at closing . . . . $ _____
   B. Sum of all financing described in the attached: ☐ Third Party Financing Addendum, ☐ Loan Assumption Addendum, ☐ Seller Financing Addendum . . . . $ _____
   C. Sales Price (Sum of A and B). . . . . $ _____

When trying to figure out how much to offer on a home, your agent will analyze homes that have sold in the neighborhood in the past year and what is "pending" or currently under contract. They should study the listing price vs. sale price—have most homes sold over their listing price? Have they sold for less? Your real estate agent will provide their professional opinion on a price to offer and you can decide what is best.

■ Earnest Money

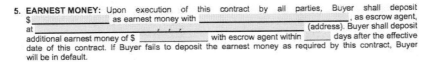

5. **EARNEST MONEY:** Upon execution of this contract by all parties, Buyer shall deposit $_____ as earnest money with _____, as escrow agent, at _____ (address). Buyer shall deposit additional earnest money of $_____ with escrow agent within ___ days after the effective date of this contract. If Buyer fails to deposit the earnest money as required by this contract, Buyer will be in default.

I briefly touched on earnest money earlier. It is one of the first action steps once your offer is accepted. When reviewing the contract, one of the pages will discuss "option period" and "earnest money." Earnest money (usually 1 to 3% of the sales price) is provided by the buyer so that the seller takes the offer seriously. You're using these funds to show the seller you're earnest about buying their house. Don't confuse this with the down payment on the house. They are two separate things. The earnest money is turned into the title company, who will hold it in an escrow account. You will lose the earnest money if you breach the contract after your option period. Otherwise, this is a deposit, and you will get it back, or it can be applied to your down payment amount at closing. Remember, you do not turn this money in until your offer is officially accepted! Make sure to have these funds available in a bank account. Your lender will need to see the paper trail! In the past, the most common way for buyers to deliver earnest money to the title company has been via check. Most recently, they have been allowing the buyer to wire this money if it's easier; who has checks anymore?!

■ Option Period

> 23. **TERMINATION OPTION:** For nominal consideration, the receipt of which is hereby acknowledged by Seller, and Buyer's agreement to pay Seller $ _____ (Option Fee) within 3 days after the effective date of this contract, Seller grants Buyer the unrestricted right to terminate this contract by giving notice of termination to Seller within _____ days after the effective date of this contract (Option Period). Notices under this paragraph must be given by 5:00 p.m. (local time where the Property is located) by the date specified. If no dollar amount is stated as the Option Fee or if Buyer fails to pay the Option Fee to Seller within the time prescribed, this paragraph will not be a part of this contract and Buyer shall not have the unrestricted right to terminate this contract. If Buyer gives notice of termination within the time prescribed, the Option Fee will not be refunded; however, any earnest money will be refunded to Buyer. The Option Fee ☐ will ☐ will not be credited to the Sales Price at closing. **Time is of the essence for this paragraph and strict compliance with the time for performance is required.**

When you go under contract on a home, the first thing you do is turn in the earnest and option money within seventy-two hours. The option period, along with the option money, buys you time to have home inspections done and negotiate any final terms or repairs with the seller, if possible. For example, if you have a seven-day option period written into the contract, you'll have seven days to have your inspection completed, try to further negotiate with the seller, or back out if you decide it's not the house for you. If you back out of the contract within those seven days, you will not get your option money back. The option money is typically only around $100-$300, and you as the buyer, get to decide what amount and the number of days. I've seen option period lengths as long as twelve days or as little as two days. It will depend on many things and can be used as a negotiation tactic if there are multiple offers. For example, shortening your option period and increasing your option money as a buyer will make your offer more appealing. Once under contract on the house, the ball is in the buyer's court, because the seller cannot back out of the contract, but the buyer can. The only way the seller could back out during the option period is if the buyer breaches the contract. So, it's crucial to turn in earnest and option money within seventy-two hours once you go under contract to keep in compliance. That's why you hire a realtor. We will make sure you stick to the deadlines of the contract!

■ Survey

C. SURVEY: The survey must be made by a registered professional land surveyor acceptable to the Title Company and Buyer's lender(s). (Check one box only)
☐ (1) Within _____ days after the effective date of this contract, Seller shall furnish to Buyer and Title Company Seller's existing survey of the Property and a Residential Real Property Affidavit promulgated by the Texas Department of Insurance (T-47 Affidavit). **If Seller fails to furnish the existing survey or affidavit within the time prescribed, Buyer shall obtain a new survey at Seller's expense no later than 3 days prior to Closing Date.** If the existing survey or affidavit is not acceptable to Title Company or Buyer's lender(s), Buyer shall obtain a new survey at ☐ Seller's ☐ Buyer's expense no later than 3 days prior to Closing Date.
☐ (2) Within _____ days after the effective date of this contract, Buyer shall obtain a new survey at Buyer's expense. Buyer is deemed to receive the survey on the date of actual receipt or the date specified in this paragraph, whichever is earlier.
☐ (3) Within _____ days after the effective date of this contract, Seller, at Seller's expense shall furnish a new survey to Buyer.
D. OBJECTIONS: Buyer may object in writing to defects, exceptions, or encumbrances to title: disclosed on the survey other than items 6A(1) through (7) above; disclosed in the Commitment other than items 6A(1) through (8) above; or which prohibit the following use or activity: _____

A survey is a document that shows a property's boundary lines to determine the exact amount of land that a homeowner owns. Surveys can reveal any known easements, or if your neighbor is encroaching on your land. Contractors can also use your survey to determine if and where you can build on to your home if you ever want to add an ADU or addition. Most often, the seller will have their original survey from when they bought their home. If this is the case, you, as the buyer, may not have to pay for a new one. If unable to locate the survey, the seller can check with the title company used when they closed on the home. In the contract, there is a section that discusses the survey and who will provide a new one if needed. A new survey can cost around $400-$800.

■ **Title Policy**

6. **TITLE POLICY AND SURVEY:**
  A. TITLE POLICY: Seller shall furnish to Buyer at ☐ Seller's ☐ Buyer's expense an owner policy of title Insurance (Title Policy) issued by _____ (Title Company) in the amount of the Sales Price, dated at or after closing, insuring Buyer against loss under the provisions of the Title Policy, subject to the promulgated exclusions (including existing building and zoning ordinances) and the following exceptions:
  (1) Restrictive covenants common to the platted subdivision in which the Property is located.
  (2) The standard printed exception for standby fees, taxes and assessments.
  (3) Liens created as part of the financing described in Paragraph 3.
  (4) Utility easements created by the dedication deed or plat of the subdivision in which the Property is located.

The title company researches your property, checks if there is any risk in the title chain (the historical transfers of title to a property from the present owner back to the first owner of the home), and suggests ways to eliminate that risk. After reviewing the property, the title company will send you a title commitment that will inform you of any restrictions, easements, or anything else affecting title. The title company is also where you will go on closing day to sign all the paperwork. Title insurance protects you as an owner from most claims and attacks on the title and is an expense usually paid for by the seller.

■ Home warranty

H. RESIDENTIAL SERVICE CONTRACTS: Buyer may purchase a residential service contract from a
residential service company licensed by from TREC. If Buyer purchases a residential service
contract, Seller shall reimburse Buyer at closing for the cost of the residential service contract
in an amount not exceeding $ _____ . Buyer should review any residential service
contract for the scope of coverage, exclusions and limitations. **The purchase of a residential
service contract is optional. Similar coverage may be purchased from various
companies authorized to do business in Texas.**

Also known as a residential service contract, a basic
home warranty plan is about $300-$600 a year. There are
different types of plans with various coverages. Usually, a
seller will provide this for a buyer for one year but it is
negotiable. Simply put, a home warranty maintains,
replaces, or repairs any part of the appliances, structural
components, electrical, plumbing, heating, or air
conditioning systems in your home caused by normal
wear and tear. Although this is a service paid for by the
seller, you as a buyer will need to pay the service fee
every time a contractor comes to your house. This fee can
be anywhere from $30-70 a trip.

■ Closing date

(Address of Property)
9. **CLOSING:**
A. The closing of the sale will be on or before _____ , _____ , or within 7
days after objections made under Paragraph 6D have been cured or waived, whichever date
is later (Closing Date). If either party fails to close the sale by the Closing Date, the non-
defaulting party may exercise the remedies contained in Paragraph 15.
B. At closing:
(1) Seller shall execute and deliver a general warranty deed conveying title to the Property
to Buyer and showing no additional exceptions to those permitted in Paragraph 6 and
furnish tax statements or certificates showing no delinquent taxes on the Property.
(2) Buyer shall pay the Sales Price in good funds acceptable to the escrow agent.
(3) Seller and Buyer shall execute and deliver any notices, statements, certificates,
affidavits, releases, loan documents and other documents reasonably required for the
closing of the sale and the issuance of the Title Policy.
(4) There will be no liens, assessments, or security interests against the Property which will
not be satisfied out of the sales proceeds unless securing the payment of any loans
assumed by Buyer and assumed loans will not be in default.
(5) If the Property is subject to a residential lease, Seller shall transfer security deposits (as
defined under §92.102, Property Code), if any, to Buyer. In such an event, Buyer shall
deliver to the tenant a signed statement acknowledging that the Buyer has acquired the

Usually, a closing will take place around thirty days after the seller accepts the buyer's offer. That's how long a lender and their team will take to sift through all of the information you've provided, have an appraisal done and officially approve you. On your closing date, you will usually go to the title company to sign all the documentation, and that is when your down payment and closing costs are to be paid. If the closing date needs to be pushed back, both the seller and buyer must be in agreement and sign an amendment to extend the closing. Also, remember you usually don't pay your first mortgage payment until about a month or more after you purchase your home. Consult your lender about this!

Contingencies

A contingency clause defines a condition or action that must be met for the contract to become binding. If you breach these contingencies, you could face losing your earnest money or even legal consequences. Common contingencies in a contract include:

Financing Contingency:
The financing contingency allocates time to obtain financing for the purchase of your home. If your lender denies your loan application, you are allowed to back out of the contract and reclaim your earnest money. If your lender gives you a preapproval letter, that typically means they think that their underwriting team will approve your loan application. But, let's say you go under contract on

the house, and within 15 days you decide to buy a car, your lender may then say, you are no longer able to purchase this home. If your financing contingency is 18 days, you can break the contract and get your earnest money back. This is just one example of how a financing contingency may help you out, but if you are already under contract, be sure to consult your lender before making any big purchases or job changes.

B. APPROVAL OF FINANCING: Approval for the financing described above will be deemed to have been obtained when Buyer Approval and Property Approval are obtained.
  1. Buyer Approval:
     ❑ This contract is subject to Buyer obtaining Buyer Approval. If Buyer cannot obtain Buyer Approval, Buyer may give written notice to Seller within _____ days after the effective date of this contract and this contract will terminate and the earnest money will be refunded to Buyer. If Buyer does not terminate the contract under this provision, the contract shall no longer be subject to the Buyer obtaining Buyer Approval. Buyer Approval will be deemed to have been obtained when (i) the terms of the loan(s) described above are available and (ii) lender determines that Buyer has satisfied all of lender's requirements related to Buyer's assets, income and credit history.
     ❑ This contract is not subject to Buyer obtaining Buyer Approval.

Appraisal Contingency:

If the property does not appraise, at or below the sales price, the contract can be terminated. In this situation, the seller would need to decrease the amount to match the appraised value, or the buyer would need to bring more cash to the table to make up the difference. If there is no agreement between both parties, the buyer can back out and should get their earnest money back. For example, you make an offer on a home for $400,000, and the appraisal comes back at $395,000. In this case, the seller would need to agree to sell their home for $395,000, or the buyer could put $5,000 more down. You and the seller could also split the difference.

2. <u>Property Approval</u>: Property Approval will be deemed to have been obtained when the Property has satisfied lender's underwriting requirements for the loan, including but not limited to appraisal, insurability, and lender required repairs. If Property Approval is not obtained, Buyer may terminate this contract by giving notice to Seller before closing and the earnest money will be refunded to Buyer.

House Sale Contingency:

If you need to sell your home before you can buy, you have the option of writing that requirement into your contract. You will need to fill out a document called the "Addendum for Sale of Other Property by Buyer."

■   Closing Costs

Closing costs are usually between two to five percent of the sales price. The seller pays the real estate agent fees, and are not considered closing costs to the buyer. Your lender should give you a good faith estimate soon after you go through the pre-approval process. The fees that go into your closing costs will vary. Typical closing costs include:

- Loan origination fees
- Appraisal
- Survey (If a new one is needed)
- Underwriting fees
- Title search fees and title insurance.
- Prepaid taxes
- Attorney fee
- Application fee

Step #5. Yay! Offer Accepted.

Below is a list of immediate steps that a buyer usually goes through once their offer is accepted. As a reference, I answer the question, "How to Make an Offer in Austin's Hot Market," in the "Common Questions and Concerns" section of this guide on page 51.

Offer accepted:

1. Turn in your Option and Earnest money checks within seventy two hours after the effective contract date. Option money goes to the seller, and earnest money goes to the title company and will sit in an escrow account until closing day.

2. Schedule the inspection within your option period, so that you have time to get to know your house a bit before moving forward. This also gives you time to terminate the contract if you don't like what the inspector finds.

3. Review inspection report and start negotiations with the seller if needed. The repairs don't need to be completed within the option period. But there needs to be a final agreement made before the option period is up.

4. Settle negotiations with an amendment. An amendment is a document that makes a change to the contract. For example, the inspector sends his final report,

How To Buy A House In Austin : Kristina Modares

and you pick three items you want to be repaired by the seller: 1.) The water heater, 2.) A few rotting shingles on the roof, and 3.) To have the insulate attic insulated. You present your list to the seller, and they agree to fix only two repairs: shingles, and the water heater. After considering your options, you decide you're happy with this compromise. Your agent would write this in an amendment, and both the seller and buyer would sign. These repairs must be agreed upon within the option period. **Remember, the repairs will need to be done before closing, not before your option period is up.** This should give the seller plenty of time to make arrangements. Buyers can also ask for money in lieu of repairs; many sellers prefer this route.

Inspection:

As soon as your offer is accepted, you should schedule an inspection. Your real estate agent will assist you with this process. The inspection should be completed within your option period, so there will be time to make further negotiations. Remember, in Austin, the option period is usually between five to seven days. Inspections can last a few hours, but I always encourage my buyers to come at the end so the inspector can go over the report with them. It's a great way to start getting to know your home. The inspector is looking for things you may not have noticed before. The report can be twenty to forty pages, but don't be alarmed; this is typical. Your realtor will also be there and has seen many inspection reports. We will help you navigate what a serious problem is and what is pretty standard to see during an inspection.

You should receive the report by the end of the day or the following day. Your real estate agent will send the seller an amendment with the repairs you would like to have fixed. You can also negotiate for money instead of repairs. Buyers need to be mindful of the option period and be sure to make all necessary negotiations within this time frame. If you back out of the contract within your option period, you will get back your earnest money back but lose your option money as well as the cost of an inspection. The cost of a basic inspection usually starts at around $300.

Appraisal:

After negotiations have concluded, the next major hurdle is the appraisal. Your lender will hire an appraiser to ensure the property is enough to cover a loan in case you stop making payments. The appraiser researches similar homes in your area and compares recent sales to determine the market value of the house. Let's say you put an offer on a home in a neighborhood that has recently gone up in value. You love the home and submit a full price offer of $380,000. You go through the inspection, and your option period ends. Everything is going well, but then the appraiser comes out and decides the home doesn't appraise for $380,000. The appraiser has looked at other homes in the neighborhood and can't find comparables that justify the price you offered. The appraiser thinks it's worth $370,000. Their conclusion will lead to more negotiations between you and the seller. There's a $10,000 difference between the initial $380K and valued $370K. There are a few options. 1.) The seller will agree to lower the selling price to $370K, 2.) the buyer will come up with the $10,000 in cash, or 3.) the seller will lower the cost slightly, and the buyer will come up with the rest in cash. Sometimes, this can be a deal-breaker, especially if the seller has no intention of lowering the initial price, and the buyer doesn't have enough to make up the difference. The seller may then go with a backup offer or put the home back on the market. In my experience as a realtor, in this current market, I have only run into this problem a few times!

Dang! Back to the Drawing Board.

Your offer may not be accepted. Don't let it discourage you! There are many reasons it could be rejected and there will be more homes. Dust yourself off and try again.

Step #6. Pre-closure: I See the Light!

After you get through these steps, the rest of the transaction should go relatively smooth. The title company will run a full title search of the property, and your lender will be working towards final loan approval. Since you'll be preparing for closing, you still may have some more paperwork to review or fill out:

Title Commitment:

This discloses any liens or defects that affect your future home. Make sure to look through the document completely, paying particular attention to:

- **Schedule A** of the title commitment. This identifies the current owner and the legal description.
- **Schedule B** of the commitment. This identifies if there are any easements, mineral reservations, and restrictions that won't be covered by your policy.
- **Schedule C** of the commitment. This lets you know if there are any requirements that you must meet before closing. Typical examples include paying off liens or resolving ownership problems.

Homeowners Insurance:

If your personal property is damaged or destroyed by an event covered by your policy, homeowners insurance will pay for your losses. If you're like most Americans and need to finance your home (if you're not paying cash), your lender will more than likely require that you purchase at least some homeowners insurance before you can close on your home. To learn more about homeowners insurance rates in Austin, Texas, you can visit the Texas department of insurance website.

Step #7. Final Walk Through: The Home Stretch!

Before closing, your agent will schedule a final walk-through of the home. During the walk-through, you and your agent will check to make sure everything is repaired and in its proper place.

At least three days before close, you will receive your closing disclosure from your lender. This document will go over your loan details: loan terms, monthly payments, and a breakdown of your closing costs. Your closing disclosure shows the final amount of money you will need to bring to the title company on the day you close. Buyers may wire transfer funds or bring a cashiers check to the title company. You'll have to check with the title company to see what they prefer. If you wire money, be wary of wire fraud! You'd be surprised how well hackers can imitate title companies or even your realtor. Also, double-check with your realtor or the title company before sending any funds!

Step #8. Closing Time.

Closing is typically held at the title company. As soon as the title company has the loan documents from the lender, they'll let you know the final amount needed for closing, through the closing disclosure. Then you can initiate the wire transfer either the day before closing or the morning of or bring in a cashiers check. Don't forget to start switching over utilities and changing your address wherever needed. On closing day, you will need to sign many documents, and it usually takes about an hour. The title company will have one of their escrow agents go over each document as you sign. Your agent will often come for moral support. I bring clients gifts on this day and tell them about the support we offer after they become a homeowner. The seller typically closes on the same day, but at a different time, you won't come into contact with them. Your title company, lender, and the seller and buyer agents work hard to close on time, but sometimes, your lender may need an extension. This can be anywhere from a few days to a week and is simply done through an amendment document.

Step #9. Celebrate!

You just bought a home in Austin, and that is cause for celebration. There are so many fun things to get out and do in this city: grab a drink, ride your bike, or combine the two because apparently, that's a thing here. There is something in this amazing town that caters to almost everyone. Celebrate however your heart desires! Remember, if we are your agents, we don't go away after you officially become a homeowner. You will have us to help answer questions throughout the year. We also created a homeowner's Facebook group for our clients. This allows you to share information and ask questions with fellow first-time buyers and your real estate agent.

Common Questions & Concerns

Phew, okay, we went over a lot in the previous section. The following questions and answers section is my **favorite part of the guide**. It will clear up a lot of common misconceptions and confusion that can arise when talking about buying a home. I go over topics such as agent commission, HOA's & deed restrictions, buying vs. renting, and much more.

How Much Do I Pay My Real Estate Agent?

If you're buying a home, you don't pay your realtor. You should definitely have an expert guide you through the process and look out for your best interests. A real estate agent is held by law to owe specific duties to their client. When a seller lists a home, he/she makes an agreement that the agent will be paid (typically) 6 percent of the sales price of the home in commission. Half of this will go to the agent who brings a buyer. Most agents must then pay their brokerage a cut of their commission and put aside a percentage for taxes.

How Much Money Will I Need?

Although this is a job for your lender, I can tell you a few of the costs you will need to consider.

Cash to close: Cash to close is the amount of money you bring to closing, which includes your **down payment, closing costs**, and escrows for **property taxes** and **homeowners insurance**.

The following costs will be due on the day you close. Your title company will help set up closing and money wiring.

Down payment:
- Typically around 3-20% of the sales price

- Example: If you bought a home for $350,000, your down payment could be anywhere from $10,500 to $70,000.
- Your lender will help you decide what makes the most sense for you financially.

Closing costs:
- Typically around 2-5% of the sales price
- Prepaids: These are costs associated with your home that need to be paid in advance when getting a loan that will accrue between the closing date and month-end.
- Property Taxes
- Homeowner's Insurance
- Mortgage Interest
- Other Potential Costs:
  - Appraisal Fee
  - Credit Report Fee
  - Loan Origination Charge
  - Title Services & Lender's Title Insurance Fees
  - Owner's Title Insurance
  - Recording Charges
  - Wire Transfer Fee
  - Prepaid Mortgage Interest
  - Property Taxes
  - Prorated Taxes
  - Homeowners Insurance Reserves

Why Do I Keep Hearing I Need a 20 Percent Down Payment?

When purchasing a property, the majority of the population won't pay for a house in all cash and must go through a local lender or bank to borrow money. Buyers then need to consider how much money should be used as a down payment. When I was growing up, my dad always told me it was best to have no less than a 20 percent down payment. His argument was he didn't want to pay PMI (Private Mortgage Insurance). That cost is typically 0.5 to 1.0 percent of the loan amount and is charged to a buyer who puts less than 20 percent down on their home. So, if your loan amount were $100,000, meaning you're borrowing $100,000, you would pay at most $1,000 a year extra for PMI if you put less than 20 percent for a down payment. Consider your situation. Do you want to tie up that much money—a 20 percent down payment? Or, is that your rainy-day fund? Think about how "liquid" you need your cash to be. Paying a 3 to 15 percent down payment may not be so bad! Think of the risk vs. return. Your lender will be the best resource to figure out what's right for you.

Should I Buy or Rent?

Many discuss rising home costs in Austin, but rent is also going up. So, what is rent? Money you are never going to see again. If you're financially capable of buying and planning to live in Austin for at least a couple of years, more often than not, it makes sense for you to buy. If you want to lower your monthly payment, you may consider getting a roommate, adding an ADU, or utilizing Airbnb, or short-term rentals programs like Homads.

How Do I Make an Offer in Austin's "Hot Market"?

In Austin's competitive market, be prepared to make moves quickly if you want a home in a popular neighborhood.

There can be multiple reasons a seller chooses another offer over yours, and you can never know exactly what the seller is thinking or know who your competition is. One of the tricks I tell my clients is to write a note to the seller, explaining why you will love and cherish their home and attach a picture of yourself. This could put you ahead of the competition! You must put in the effort to make this "business transaction" more personal. It isn't just money and cement; it's your future home. Maybe you will raise kids here! Maybe you will grow old here! The seller may not care, but it could tug their heartstrings. **That said, no matter how much you play on the seller's emotions, you won't win a bidding war with a low-ball offer and a cute picture of your family.** You need to be a strong buyer and also add a few personal touches to make yourself relatable and more than just a source of cash.

In Austin, while you need to be prepared to pay full price or over asking price, **don't assume you will always do this**. A lot of sellers get caught up in the hype they hear about Austin's hot market, and they may think they can list their home for over market value. These homes will not sell quickly, and these homes will not be sold for over the asking price, or even near the asking price! Properties that will go into multiple offer situations are priced according to market value and in high demand neighborhoods.

When you put an offer on a home, it may be a good idea for your loan officer (lender) to call the seller's agent, not only as a friendly introduction but to also reassure the seller's real estate agent that you're a qualified buyer. There are a lot of "over promise, under deliver" situations that can often occur with banks and lenders. If a potential buyer's lender is the type of person to call and communicate well with me—major brownie points in my book! Everybody wants a smooth and easy transaction, and this will happen with a team who communicates well and often.

Other tactics to consider if you are in a multiple offer situation are:
- Shortening your option period.
- Using conventional loan instead of FHA loan (Federal Housing Administration).
  - This will be discussed in more detail further along.

- A quicker close. Make sure to clear this with your lender first.
- Getting "conditionally approved" and waiving your financing contingency in your offer. Discuss this with your lender first.
- Don't ask the seller to pay for closing costs.
- Offering over list price.

How Can I Breach a Contract and Possibly Lose my Earnest Money?

- If you waive your contingencies
  - By waiving your financing contingency, when submitting an offer, you are stating that you do not need or expect a refund if your lender does not approve funding.
- If you ignored crucial dates in the contract
  - Items to look over in your contract that have dates attached to them include: option period, financing, title, survey, and seller's disclosure.
- If you randomly decide, *nah, this home isn't for me*.
  - If there's nothing wrong with the property or your financing, and you are past your option period, chances are you're NOT getting that earnest money back.

Why a Seller May Be Hesitant with FHA Buyers?

An FHA loan is government-backed and allows people to buy a home with a down payment as low as 3.5 percent. Unlike a conventional loan, with FHA, you need to meet two sets of qualification criteria: the lender's criteria AND the government's. By insuring the mortgage, the government is guaranteeing that the lender will be repaid even if the borrower defaults on the loan. This program can be great for people who otherwise may not be able to afford to buy a home. If you are an FHA buyer making an offer on a home in a popular area, it will be crucial for your lender to call the sellers agent to reassure them that you're qualified. A seller and their realtor may be concerned that an FHA deal may fall through because of finances.

When a seller and an agent review multiple offers, a buyer's financing is considered upfront. A better loan is a better offer. If all the other contingencies are equal, a better loan has the best chance of closing. All FHA concerns mainly stem from these questions: Will this person be approved? Will we close on time, or at all?

Will the Seller Pay My Closing Costs in Austin?

In Austin's hot market, it may be harder to get the seller to pay your closing costs, but it depends on the area and the situation. I would recommend looking at property that's been on the market for over thirty days and checking the surrounding homes in the neighborhood. What's the average amount of time they spend on the market? What's the average sales price? Below asking? You may have a shot. The worst that can happen is the seller says, "No." **Also, remember you always have to come up with your down payment.** This means, your agent, lender, or seller cannot help you—your family, on the other hand, may gift you the down payment money. **Anyone can gift up to $14,000 tax-free a year.**

Do All Austin HOAs Have the Same Rules?

No. In Texas, the condo contracts require that the seller discloses Homeowners Association Information to a prospective buyer after they go under contract. A buyer has the right to terminate within six days after the condominium documents and resale certificate are delivered. Your real estate agent can help answer some of the questions about the HOA before you go under contract. **Remember, your option period is a way to pull out of the contract no matter what. The only penalty is losing your option money check.**

What are Deed Restrictions?

When you buy a home, there may be certain conditions that prohibit you from doing certain things. These stipulations are known as deed restrictions. Properties that don't have an HOA still have deed restrictions, but the enforcement may not be as strict as it would be with an

HOA. In short, your neighbor would have to hire a lawyer to enforce something. Common deed restrictions include:

- How or if you can rent out your home.

- The number of rooms you can add on.

- Landscaping: what you can plant or how you maintain your lawn.

- The style of homes allowed.

- If you can run a business from home.

- Rules about pets.

- Exterior paint colors.

- Fees for road maintenance or amenities.

Building a Custom Home

When it comes to building a home, finding the right lot may seem like a chore. What many people don't realize is that sometimes builders own multiple lots in many different neighborhoods. They may even have access to "unlisted" lots through their neighborhood relationships. It's very important to find reputable builders. A few important things to know about your builder:

- How many homes is the builder working on at once? How are the projects managed?

- How many homes does the builder complete in a year? Include start and completion times.

- Does the builder use the same sub-contractors?

- How does the builder bid your homes? Fixed cost? Cost plus?

- How is client communication handled through the process?

And many more! Your real estate agent will help you pick the right builder for your wants and needs. It's very important to have them by your side to make sure timelines are being met, and somebody is looking out for your best interests.

Does Austin Have High Property Taxes?

Yes, we do...HOWEVER, Austin doesn't have state income tax. Most find that with the higher property taxes it comes out to be about the same. The **2.1 to 2.4 percent** range is a pretty **average tax rate** for Austin, but it can be anywhere between 1.8 to 3.3 percent. You often see 3 percent or more in new developments; usually this is tacked on toward the infrastructure of the development. You can find out how much you will pay in yearly taxes by multiplying the tax rate by the sale price. If you use our **home search**, there is a mortgage calculator built in that will show you what your mortgage payment is, including the tax rate. Remember, your monthly mortgage payment includes principal, interest, homeowners insurance, and property taxes. To access our home search, head to OpenHouseAustin.co and "search homes".

What Are The "First Time Buyer Benefits"?

You can take up to $10,000 from your IRA without a penalty for early withdrawal, and a couple can use $20,000 combined.

The city of Austin's has a few first-time buyer programs that you may be eligible for. They can assist with your down payment and possibly closing costs. You can check AustinTexas.gov for more information.

Even if you have owned a home before, you may still be eligible for first-time buyer benefits. For example, the federal government's definition of a first-time homebuyer is someone who hasn't owned a personal residence in the past three years.

Common Homestead Exemptions?

You can lower your taxes each year if you file an exemption on your primary residence. The only thing you need is a photo ID and proof of residence, and an application from your county of residence. It's free to apply, and the deadline is April 30th, but you must've lived in your home as of January 1st of the tax year for which you're applying, to be eligible.

Another common tax exemption is a home sale exclusion. To qualify, you need to live in your primary residence for at least two years out of the five years leading up to the sale. Up to $250,000 of profit from the sale of your home can be tax-free; $500,000 if you are married.

Some people avoid paying capital gains tax on their home by doing a 1031 exchange. This is when you use the proceeds from your house to buy another house that is of equal or greater value of the home you're selling.

Austin Activity Starter Kit

Ah, Austin. The place where dogs are treated as children, winters are a joke, and there's a constant battle between staying fit and stuffing your face full of spectacular food. I wanted to include a few of the places I loved when I first moved to Austin and still enjoy today! There are so many great places in this city but this is a great starter kit if you've never been before.

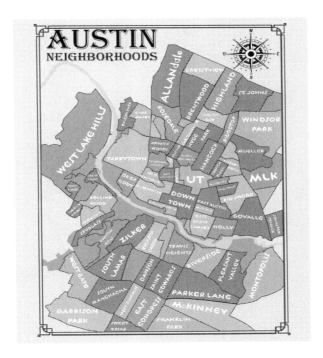

Favorite Day trips

McKinney Falls: About a 15 minute drive from Austin, 9.6 miles. Camp, hike, mountain or road bike and bouldering. You can also fish and swim in Onion Creek.

Lake Travis: About a 40 minute drive from Austin, 22 miles. Boating, fishing, swimming, parasailing and zip lining.

Hamilton Pool: About a 45 minute drive from Austin, 30 miles. Swimming, fishing, hiking, basketball, volleyball, tennis courts, disc golf course.

Gruene: About a 50 minute drive from Austin, 46 miles. Float the river, Gruene dance hall, the Gristmill, wineries and shopping.

Fredericksburg: About a 1 hour and 30 minutes drive from Austin, 78 miles. Wineries, German food, historic walking tours, shopping, hiking, site seeing.

Enchanted Rock: About a 2 hour drive from Austin, 96 miles. Hike, backpack, camp, rock climb.

Favorite Local Activities

This is a list of my personal favorite things to do in Austin.

1. Grab a dog for a day from Austin Pets Alive and walk on Lady Bird Lake. The shelter runs a program that allows people to take dogs for much needed walks on the trail.
2. Paddle board on Lady Bird Lake.
3. Enjoy an amazing dinner at Sway on a weekday, it's less crowded! I definitely recommend Tom Kha Gai (coconut & chicken soup) & crab fried rice.
4. Work from Radio coffee's outdoor patio. LeverCraft Coffee is another new favorite coffee shop.
5. Check out a new musician at Whip-In or One-To-One.
6. Go to Broken Spoke and watch adorable older couples two-step...go to The White Horse and possibly partake in two-stepping with hipsters, cowboys, the young and middle aged.
7. Go to the Alamo Drafthouse, and slurp on a boozy milkshake. Also, Violet Crown is amazing for unique movies.
8. Try out the Austin Bouldering Project. I'm not a rock climber, and I did this successfully. Trust me, you don't need to be experienced!
9. Fonda San Miguel brunch. This is a tad pricey but they have a super amazing spread. A personal favorite for dinner as well.
10. The Nightowls at Icenhauer's on Sundays. Drinks. Rainey Street. Motown Music. Dancing.

Ready To Take The Next Steps?

Thank you for reading **How to Buy a House in Austin**. I truly hope this has been helpful to you and you now feel comfortable about the home buying process!

Do you want...
To jump on a consultation call?
To attend a workshop or have us come to your office?
A list of reputable lenders?
To be set up with a home search?
Email us at <u>OpenHouseAustinGroup@RealtyAustin.com</u>

Kristina Modares
Co-Founder of Open House Austin
3307 Oak Spring Dr. Austin, TX 78721
OpenHouseAustin.co

@OpenHouse_Austin

References

The Buying Process. (n.d.). Retrieved from https://www.texasrealestate.com/for-buyers-sellers-renters/the-buying-process

TREC - Forms, Laws, Contracts Main Page. (n.d.). Retrieved from https://www.trec.state.tx.us/formslawscontracts/default.asp

Austin Real Estate Report. (n.d.). Retrieved from http://www.austinhomesearch.com/pages/austin-market-update

Austin Neighborhood Guide. (n.d.). Retrieved from https://www.austinhomelistings.com/austin-neighborhoods.php

"Tips for Buying a Home in Austin." *Austin Real Estate.*(n.d.). Retrieved from http://www.austinhomesearch.com/pages/tools/tips-for-buying-a-home-in-austin

"Appraisals and Appraised Value." *Mortgage*. (n.d.). Retrieved from http://www.thetruthaboutmortgage.com/appraisals-and-appraised-value

"February 2016 Market Report - The Austin Board of REALTORS®." *The Austin Board of REALTORS*. N.p. Web.

Notes

My Real Estate Team:

Realtor:

Lender:

My Home Buying Criteria:

Number of Bed/Bath:

Area:

Size:

Deal Breakers:

Anything Else?:

Notes

Notes

**Remember to start thinking about how much you want your mortgage payment to be! How much money are you going to put down? Your lender can help you figure out what's best for you!

Notes

Notes